This book was made by Robert Tainsh,
Simon Mugford and Louise Rupnik.

Copyright © 2006 St. Martin's Press

Published by priddy ☺ books
4 Crinan Street, London, N1 9XW
A division of Macmillan Publishers Ltd.
Manufactured in China

www.priddybooks.com

My Little
Picture Dictionary

apple

This **apple** is crisp, crunchy and very tasty to eat.

paint

I like to **paint** pictures, so my favourite class at school is art.

watch

I checked my **watch** to see if I was late.

Roger Priddy

priddy books
big ideas for little people

Aa

above

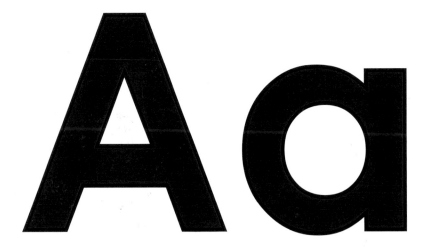

address

The bird is flying in the sky, high **above** the ground.

above higher up, over

4 Crinan Street,
London,
N1 9XW

The **address** is written on the front of the envelope.

address details of where someone lives

aeroplane

We looked up and saw a red **aeroplane** flying in the sky.

aeroplane machine with wings that flies

all

All of the girls in this picture are sitting on chairs.

all the whole amount

alphabet

A B C D E F
G H I J K L M
N O P Q R S T
U V W X Y Z

Our **alphabet** contains 26 letters from A to Z.

alphabet set of letters in a fixed order

ambulance

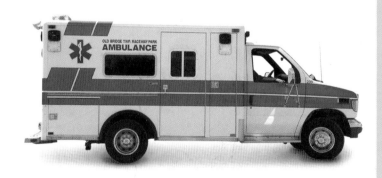

The **ambulance** has flashing lights and a loud siren.

ambulance vehicle that carries sick people

and

Clare **and** Rose have been friends since they were four years old.

and in addition to

angry

Mark's face screws up and turns red when he is **angry.**

angry feeling very upset

animals

Here are four different **animals.** Do you know what they are?

animals living creatures

ant

I found this **ant** in my kitchen crawling on the floor.

ant small insect that lives in underground nests

apple

This **apple** is crisp, crunchy
and very tasty to eat.

apple round firm fruit that grows on trees

argue

Kate and Bobby **argue** about
which TV programme to watch.

argue disagree with someone angrily

arms

Peter is showing us how
strong his **arms** are.

arms parts between your shoulders and hands

astronaut

The **astronaut** wears a special
suit for a spacewalk.

astronaut someone who travels in space

Bb

baby

Nate is a very happy **baby,** who loves to crawl around.

baby newly born or very young child

back

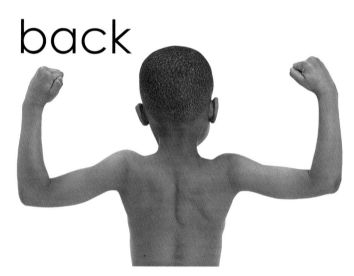

Peter has turned around and he is showing us his **back.**

back the rear part of your upper body

bake

Amanda is making a tasty cake mix to **bake.**

bake to cook by heating in an oven

ball

Sam is heading the **ball** to practise his soccer skills.

ball round object used in games

balloons

We are having a party and need to put up some **balloons.**

balloons rubber bags that can be filled with air

bananas

Bananas grow on trees in bunches called 'hands'.

bananas yellow, curved tropical fruit

barn

[baːn] sto doka, oboome

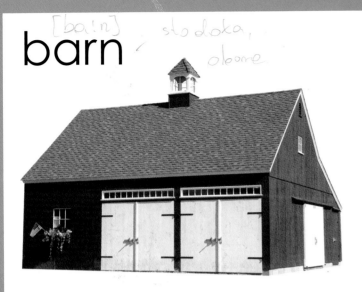

The farmer puts the animals
in the **barn** at night.

barn building where crops or animals are kept

bat

The **bat** hangs upside down
in a cave to sleep.

bat flying animal that comes out at night

bath

Jimmy likes to play with bubbles
and his toys in the **bath.**

bath container that you sit in to have a wash

beach

In the summer we go to
the **beach** to swim.

beach strip of sand or pebbles next to water

beak

This bird is called a macaw.
It can break nuts with its **beak.**

beak hard, horny part of a bird's mouth

bear

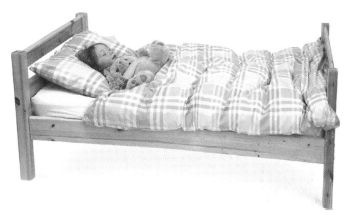

This **bear** has very sharp claws,
which he uses to catch fish.

bear large, furry animal

beautiful

Laura likes to dress up as a
beautiful princess.

beautiful very pretty

bed

At night when I am tired,
it is time to go to **bed.**

bed piece of furniture that you sleep in

bee

The **bee** flies to the pretty flower to collect some nectar.

bee a flying insect that makes honey

beetle

Look under a rock in your garden and you might find a **beetle.**

beetle a flying insect with hard wing covers

begin

Lucy is about to **begin** her ballet practice.

begin to start

behind

Lucy is having a break and she is hiding **behind** the curtain.

behind on the other side

berries

In autumn you will see colourful **berries** on some trees.

berries small fruit found on trees or bushes

between

Amanda is standing **between** Lewis and Max.

between to have things on either side

bicycle

Emma has been given a new **bicycle** for her birthday.

bicycle two-wheeled vehicle that you ride

big

Rose looks up to her dad because she is small and he is **big.**

big large or important

birds [bɜːdz]

Cockatoos, kookaburras and
parrots are all types of **birds.**

birds creatures with wings and feathers

birthday

Jodie is four years old today.
Happy **birthday** Jodie!

birthday anniversary of the day you were born

bite

Charlie takes a **bite** out of
his crunchy apple.

bite to close your teeth around something

boat

This **boat** is heading into
harbour with its catch of fish.

boat vehicle used for travelling on water

bone

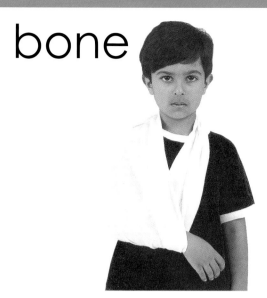

Michael has broken a **bone** in his arm, so he is wearing a sling.

bone part of a human or animal skeleton

book

Alice is reading her favourite **book** about princesses.

book pages of words and pictures

boys

These two **boys** are wearing their best shirts for a party.

boys male children

bread

What do you like to eat with a slice of **bread**?

bread food made from flour and water

break

Look out Jenny! The mugs
are about to **break.**

break damage something

breakfast

Max is eating his favourite
cereal for **breakfast.**

breakfast a meal eaten in the morning

bridge

Cars, trucks and people use
this **bridge** to cross the bay.

bridge structure that crosses a space

brother

James loves his little
brother Harry.

brother boy with the same parents as you

building

This is going to be a new **building** for people to live in.

building a structure with walls and a roof

bulldozer

The **bulldozer** is being used to build a new road.

bulldozer powerful machine for moving earth

bus

We use the **bus** to travel to the other side of town.

bus large vehicle that carries passengers

butterfly

The beautiful **butterfly** flies in the garden looking for flowers.

butterfly flying insect with large, colourful wings

Cc

cabbage

Today we ate roast chicken, potatoes and **cabbage.**

cabbage large, leafy vegetable

cakes

We ate our favourite **cakes** at the birthday party.

cakes sweet food eaten as a snack or dessert

call

Joe is using the telephone to **call** his grandma.

call to telephone someone

camel

A **camel** is used to carry people and goods across the desert.

camel mammal with one or two humps

camera

Amanda uses her new **camera** to take a picture.

camera machine that takes photographs

canoe

Daddy and I paddled the **canoe** down the river.

canoe narrow boat that you paddle

car

I cannot wait until I am old enough to drive a **car.**

car motor vehicle that carries people

carrots

My pet rabbit eats a whole bunch of **carrots** for breakfast.

carrots long, orange vegetables

cat

Cathy loves to stroke her pet **cat** Oscar.

cat small animal, often kept as a pet

catch

Tommy has thrown the ball and Alice is about to **catch** it.

catch grab something flying through the air

chair

Alannah is sitting on the **chair** and reading her book.

chair piece of furniture that you sit on

chameleon

The **chameleon** sits on a branch in the sunshine.

chameleon lizard that can change its colour

cheese

My favourite snack is a ham and **cheese** sandwich.

cheese food made from milk

cheetah — gepard

The **cheetah** is looking for a zebra to chase.

cheetah wild cat that can run very fast

chick

The chicken laid an egg and then a **chick** hatched out.

chick baby chicken

chicken

This **chicken** has laid an egg for our breakfast.

chicken a bird kept on farms

children

These four **children** are in the same class at school.

children young people

chimpanzee

If you go to the jungle, you might see a **chimpanzee.**

chimpanzee large ape from Africa

chocolate

I gave my mummy some **chocolate** for her birthday.

chocolate food made from cocoa beans

choose

Kate likes all of the kittens but has to **choose** one.

choose to pick out something

circus

Keira went to the **circus** and now she wants to be a clown.

circus travelling show

city

The **city** is a place with lots of tall buildings.

city very large town

clap

Jodie likes to **clap** along
with the music.

clap hit your hands together

clean

After Beth has a bath, she
is nice and **clean.**

clean not dirty or messy

climb

To use a slide you first have
to **climb** the steps.

climb move upwards

clock

The **clock** has a long hand
and a short hand.

clock machine that tells the time

clothes

Socks, trousers and T-shirts
are all types of **clothes.**

clothes things that you wear

clouds

You usually see fluffy **clouds**
like these on a sunny day.

clouds drops of water floating in the sky

coat

[kaʊt]

kurtka

Benjamin has put on his
coat to go out to play.

coat clothing you wear outside to keep warm

cold

This seal has a furry coat to
stop him from feeling **cold.**

cold low temperature

colours

This picture of a rainbow has
six different **colours.**

colours red, yellow, blue etc

come

Clare and Cathy want Debra
to **come** towards them.

come move towards a place

computer

Keira is playing a game
on the **computer.**

computer machine used for work and play

cook

The chef has all the ingredients
to **cook** the meal.

cook prepare and heat food to eat

cow

The **cow** eats grass in a field and goes to a shed to be milked.

cow female farm animal that makes milk

crab

We found a **crab** when we went to the beach.

crab creature with a hard shell and pincers

crocodile

The **crocodile** swims in rivers and walks on land.

crocodile big reptile with very powerful jaws

cry

Amanda was very sad and started to **cry.**

cry to shed tears

Dd

dad

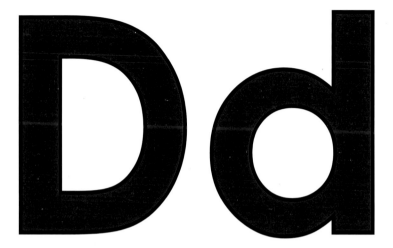

Rose and her **dad** love
each other very much.

dad name for your father

dance

Ashley goes to ballet class
where she learns to **dance**.

dance moving in time to music

day

Alannah dressed warmly
because it was a cold **day**.

day the 24 hours from midnight to midnight

deer

We saw a **deer** when we went
for a walk in the woods.

deer wild animal that can run very fast

dentist

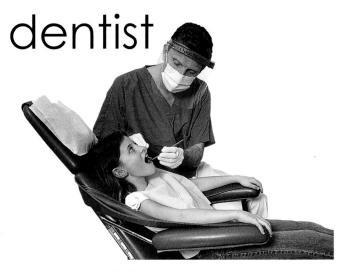

Leigh is having her teeth
checked by the **dentist**.

dentist someone who treats and cleans teeth

desert - pustynia

The sand hills in a **desert**
are called dunes.

desert very dry area with hardly any plants

dinosaur

This **dinosaur** is called Kentrosaurus.
It had rows of spikes along its back.

dinosaur prehistoric reptile that lived on land

doctor

Scott visited the **doctor**
for a check-up.

doctor someone who treats sick people

dog

This is my pet **dog** Archie.
I love him very much.

dog animal with a tail that wags, kept as a pet

dolphin

The **dolphin** is a very
intelligent creature.

dolphin water mammal with a long snout

donkey

The **donkey** has pointed
ears and says, 'ee-yaw'.

donkey animal, related to the horse

drink

Ellie was thirsty, so she
had a **drink** of water.

drink swallow liquid

dry

Jamal got wet when he had bath,
but the towel has made him **dry**.

dry not wet

ducklings

These little **ducklings** are
about two days old.

ducklings baby ducks

Ee

eagle

This **eagle** has very good eyesight and is an excellent hunter.

eagle large bird of prey

ear

Gary is pointing to his right **ear**. Can you point to your right ear?

ear part of the body used to hear

earth

The **earth** looks blue because
most of it is covered with water.

earth planet on which we live

eat

Lewis is hungry, so it is time
for him to **eat** his lunch.

eat chew and swallow food

egg

I like to eat a boiled **egg**
for breakfast.

egg object laid by birds which can be eaten

elephant

A baby **elephant** stays with its
mother until it is one year old.

elephant large animal with a trunk and tusks

empty

Josh cannot believe
the biscuit jar is **empty**!

empty if something is empty there is nothing in it

emu

The **emu** is very fast on the ground.
It can run at up to 65 km/h!

emu large bird that cannot fly

end

Joe's mummy has read to
the **end** of the story.

end the last part of something

equal

There are an **equal** number
of tarts on each plate.

equal the same amount or size

escalator

This **escalator** leads to the check-in desk at the airport.

escalator moving staircase

exercise

Alex does some stretches as part of her daily **exercise**.

exercise activity that keeps you healthy

explore

Keira has to **explore** the park as part of her nature project.

explore to look for things in a place

eyes

This funny frog has very big **eyes** to help him spot his lunch.

eyes parts used by people and animals to see

Ff

face

Alice is looking at us so we can see her pretty **face**.

face the front of your head

family

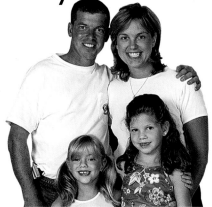

Mummy, daddy, my sister and I are part of the same **family**.

family group of people related to each other

farm

Most things that we eat
come from a **farm**.

farm place where animals live and crops grow

fast

This motorcycle has a powerful
engine that makes it go very **fast**.

fast moving quickly

feathers

This cockatoo has bright
yellow **feathers** on its head.

feathers light fluffy covering on birds

fence

Jessica had to reach through
the **fence** to get her ball.

fence something that separates areas of land

fingers

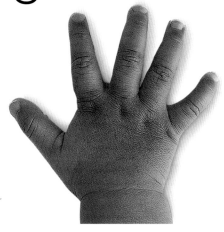

Each hand has five **fingers**.
How many do you have altogether?

fingers long parts of your hand that you move

fire engine

The firefighters keep their
fire engine clean and shiny.

fire engine machine that puts out fires

first

Melissa came **first** in
the running race.

first before something else, earliest

fish

Tropical **fish** are usually
very brightly coloured.

fish water animal with scales and fins

flag

The **flag** of the USA is called the 'Stars and Stripes'.

flag large piece of cloth with a symbol on it

flowers

I bought mummy a bunch of **flowers** when she was sick.

flowers colourful parts of plants and trees

fly

The bird spreads its wings to **fly** as it hunts for food.

fly move through the air

food

There are many different types of **food**. Which is your favourite?

food all of the things that we eat

footprint

At nursery I made a painting
with my **footprint**.

footprint mark made by a foot or shoe

forest

The **forest** is a beautiful place
to walk on a spring morning.

forest place where lots of trees grow

fox

You might find a **fox** looking
for food in your rubbish.

fox wild animal, like a dog with a bushy tail

friends

Paul and Oliver are **friends**
who go to the same school.

friends people who like each other very much

frog

This **frog** has bright red eyes
and feet with suction pads.

frog animal with webbed feet that jumps high

fruit

Fruit is tasty and good for you.
Which is your favourite?

fruit edible part of plants and trees

full

Anthony had so many toys
that his toy box was **full**.

full if something is full, there is no room left in it

fun

Kelly and Anna had a **fun**
water fight after school.

fun enjoyable, good

Gg

game

The girls enjoyed playing their favourite **game**.

game activity that you play with other people

giraffe

The **giraffe** bent down at the lake for a drink of water.

giraffe animal with a very long neck

girls

These three **girls** are dancing
along to some music.

girls female children

give

On birthdays, we **give** a present to
the person whose birthday it is.

give to hand something to another person

glasses

Heidi is wearing her
brand new **glasses**.

glasses lenses worn to help you see better

goat

The **goat** has a woolly coat and a
little beard under his chin.

goat farm animal with horns

goldfish

My **goldfish** is named Freddie.
He likes to swim around his tank.

goldfish orange-coloured fish, kept as a pet

golf

The aim of **golf** is to hit a ball
into a hole in the ground.

golf outdoor game played with a club

good

Cathy is patting Barney because
he has been a **good** dog.

good deserving praise

goose

This **goose** lives on the farm
and makes lots of noise.

goose long-necked bird that flies and swims

gorilla

This **gorilla** lives in the mountains and jungles of Africa.

gorilla very large and strong ape

grapes

Grapes can be eaten fresh, dried to make raisins, or used to make wine.

grapes small fruit that grows on vines

grass

In the summer when it is hot, I like to walk on the cool **grass**.

grass green plant that is used to make lawns

gymnast

Katherine wants to be a **gymnast**, so she practises every day.

gymnast person who does special exercises

Hh

hair

Skye has brown **hair** that goes down to her shoulders.

hair soft covering on your head

half

This apple has been chopped in **half** so that you can see the seeds.

half one of two equal parts

happy

Hayley got an A in her class and she was very **happy**.

happy to be very pleased

hat

It was a cold day, so Michael wore a warm **hat**.

hat item of clothing you wear on your head

head

Cathy helped her friends to practise standing on their **heads**.

head the top part of your body

heart

William can listen to his **heart** beating in his chest.

heart organ that pumps blood around the body

helicopter

This **helicopter** is used by the
police to chase criminals.

helicopter flying machine with spinning blades

help

"Hey," said James, "let me
help you with those books."

help to make someone's job easier

hide

It was Helen's turn to **hide**
behind the chair.

hide to go where you cannot be seen

hill

We climbed to the top of
this **hill** on our trek.

hill hump in the land, smaller than a mountain

hippopotamus   horse

The **hippopotamus** spends most
of its time wallowing in water.

hippopotamus large animal with thick skin

This **horse** is named Tommy.
He likes to go for a gallop.

horse large, strong animal that people ride

house   hug

This is the **house** at the
end of our street.

house building where people live

Vicki and Sophie gave
each other a big **hug**.

hug hold someone in a loving way

Ii

iceberg

Most of the ice in an **iceberg** floats beneath the water.

iceberg large chunk of ice floating in the sea

ice cream

On a hot day, Kelly and Anna ate some **ice cream**.

ice cream sweet frozen food

iguana

The **iguana** spends most of
its time living in trees.

iguana large lizard with a long tail

insects

Beetles, butterflies and ladybirds
are all types of **insects**.

insects small animals with six legs

inside

Jodie has been given a present.
I wonder what's **inside**?

inside within, surrounded by something

island

This **island** looks very beautiful,
but would you like to live there?

island piece of land surrounded by water

Jj

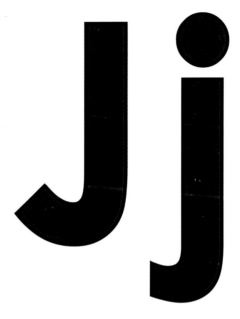

jellyfish

Some **jellyfish** have stinging tentacles that are very poisonous.

jellyfish sea creature with soft, jelly-like body

jewellery

Earrings and necklaces are types of **jewellery**.

jewellery pretty objects that you wear

jigsaw puzzle

On a rainy day I like to try
doing a **jigsaw puzzle**.

jigsaw puzzle jumbled picture puzzle to recreate

juice

Kelly and Anna needed some lemon
juice to make their lemonade.

juice liquid that comes from fruit or vegetables

jump

The girls did the highest **jump**
they could manage.

jump to leap off the ground

jungle

Lots of amazing plants and animals
can be found in the **jungle**.

jungle forest that is very hot and wet

Kk

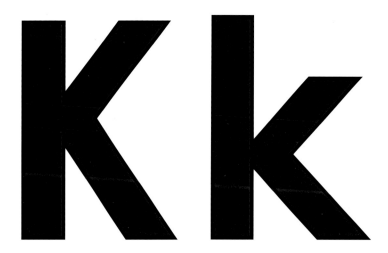

kangaroo

The female **kangaroo** keeps her baby in a pouch on her front.

kangaroo Australian animal that jumps high

karate

Jonathan and Kasey practised **karate** together.

karate fighting sport that uses chops and kicks

kick

Lewis learned how to **kick** the
ball at soccer practice.

kick to hit out with your foot

kiss

Louise planted a big **kiss**
on Gary's cheek.

kiss to touch someone with your lips

Kite

When it is windy, I go to the
park to fly my **kite**.

kite flying toy that you play with in wind

kitten

Carrie was given a very cute
kitten for her birthday.

kitten baby cat

Ll

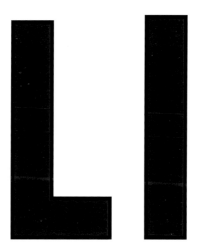

ladybird

The **ladybird** is my favourite insect, because I love its spots.

ladybird small red insect with black spots

lambs

In spring you will see newborn **lambs** leaping in the fields.

lambs baby sheep

laugh

Lilly heard a funny joke and
she began to **laugh**.

laugh make a sound that shows you are happy

leaf

This **leaf** has fallen from
a maple tree.

leaf flat, green part of a plant

left

This arrow is pointing
to the **left**.

left the opposite of right

leg

Monica is standing on
her left **leg**.

leg body part between your hip and your foot

lemon

Some drinks taste better when you add a slice of **lemon**.

lemon sour tasting fruit with a yellow skin

lick

Charlie could not wait to **lick** his lollipop.

lick to touch something with your tongue

lion

The **lion** likes to spend hours sleeping in the sun.

lion large African wild cat

listen

"I'm going to tell you a secret, so **listen** carefully."

listen to pay attention as you hear something

lizard

Some people like to keep
a **lizard** as a pet.

lizard reptile with a long body and tail

look

The girls had a **look** to see
who was coming.

look to use your eyes to see things

love

Rose and Kate **love** their
pet rabbits very much.

love to like someone or something very much

lunch

I will usually eat sandwiches
for my **lunch**.

lunch meal eaten in the middle of the day

Mm

magnifying glass

Thomas used his **magnifying glass** for school projects.

magnifying glass lens that makes things look big

make

Anna likes to **make** Christmas presents for her friends.

make to build or create something

mammal

Cows are a type of **mammal**.
A baby cow is called a calf.

mammal animal that feeds on its mother's milk

man

This **man** is my dad.
I love him very much.

man adult male person

maths

$$2 + 2 = 4$$

$$3 - 1 = 2$$

I had to practise addition and
subtraction for my **maths** homework.

math study of numbers, shapes and sizes

mechanic

The **mechanic** checked the
engine to see what was wrong.

mechanic someone who repairs cars

medicine

Karen has to take her **medicine** four times a day.

medicine something that you take if you are ill

metal

This big car is made with a lot of **metal**.

metal hard material such as steel or copper

middle

Emma stood in the **middle** of the ring during the game.

middle the centre of something

milk

Joe likes to drink a glass of **milk** before he goes to bed.

milk white liquid from animals that we drink

mirror

Princess Laura checked in the
mirror to see how pretty she is.

mirror special glass that reflects your image

money

Different types of **money** are
used in different countries.

money coins and notes we use to buy things

monkey

This squirrel **monkey** is very
good at climbing trees.

monkey furry animal with long arms and a tail

moon

The **moon** is the brightest
thing in the night sky.

moon the satellite that moves around earth

moth

This **moth** has a pattern on its back
that looks like a pair of eyes.

moth insect like a butterfly that flies at night

mother

Rosanna is the **mother**
of three girls.

mother female parent

motorcycle

This police **motorcycle** is used
to keep the our roads safe.

motorcycle two-wheeled motor vehicle

mountain

It is usually very cold at the
top of a **mountain**.

mountain very high piece of land

mouse

Some people like to keep
a **mouse** as a pet.

mouse small, furry animal with a long tail

mouth

You use your **mouth** to
eat and speak.

mouth part of your face where your teeth are

mushroom

This type of **mushroom** can be
eaten, but some are poisonous.

mushroom plant with no leaves, flowers or roots

musician

Kasey is a **musician**.
Her favourite instrument is the violin.

musician someone who plays music

Nn

nest
– gniazdo

A cuckoo will lay its eggs
in another bird's **nest**.

nest a place built by birds to lay their eggs

new

Kate has been given a **new**
scooter for her birthday.

new just bought or made

night

The buildings in the city
are lit up at **night**.

night the time between sunset and sunrise

noise

Freddie is making a lot of
noise with his toy drum.

noise a sound, especially a loud one

nose

Gary is pointing to his **nose**
with his left hand.

nose part of your face you use to smell

nurse

The **nurse** listened to
Nicole breathing.

nurse person who looks after people in hospital

ocean

octopus

I love to listen to the **ocean** waves crashing against the shore.

ocean very large area of sea

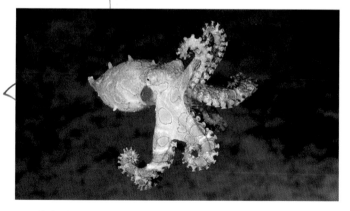

This blue-ringed **octopus** is one of the world's most poisonous creatures

octopus sea animal with eight tentacles

odd

These are **odd** socks because
they are different colours.

odd different, not matching

old

Cathy's teddy is
well-loved and very **old**.

old something that has existed for a long time

onions

My eyes start to water when
I am peeling **onions**.

onions vegetables with a very strong taste

open

Somebody has left the door
to the toy cupboard **open**.

open not closed or shut

opposite

The frog is small and the elephant is big – they are **opposite**.

opposite completely different

orange

My favourite fruit is the **orange**. I like to drink the juice.

orange round, sweet juicy fruit

orangutan

The **orangutan** has rusty orange-coloured fur.

orangutan large furry ape with strong arms

orchard

There are lots of apple trees growing in this **orchard**.

orchard field where fruit trees grow

ostrich

The **ostrich** is a bird which sometimes
buries its head in the sand.

ostrich large African bird that cannot fly

otter

This **otter** is eating its favourite
lunch – a tasty fresh fish.

otter furry animal that lives near water

over

Anna is jumping **over** her
friend Kelly.

over above, on top of something

owl

An **owl** has excellent eyesight
and can hunt for food at night.

owl bird with a large head and big eyes

Pp

paint

I like to **paint** pictures, so my favourite class at school is art.

paint to make pictures using a brush and paint

pair

Ralph is a soccer goalkeeper. He wears a **pair** of special gloves.

pair two things that go together, or match

panda

The **panda** is very rare.
Its favourite food is bamboo shoots.

panda large animal with black and white fur

paper

Paper is usually white,
but it can be any colour.

paper material that you use to write on

parrot

A **parrot** can be kept as a pet.
Some parrots can repeat words.

parrot tropical bird with a curved beak

party

Everybody had a good time
at Jodie's birthday **party**.

party time when people celebrate something

pea

I like to eat a **pea** straight
from the pod.

pea small, round, green vegetable

peach

A **peach** has very soft, furry
skin and a stone in the middle.

peach sweet, juicy fruit

pear

A **pear** grows on a tree and
it has seeds in the middle.

pear fruit that narrows towards one end

pencils

I keep my colouring **pencils**
in my school bag.

pencils tool used to write and draw

penguins

Most **penguins** live near the
South Pole where it is very cold.

penguins sea birds that cannot fly

people

These **people** are all members
of the same family.

people men, women and children

pet

Polly is Graham's **pet**. He takes
her for a walk every day.

pet animal that you take care of at home

photographer

This **photographer** took some
of the pictures in this book.

photographer person who takes photographs

picnic

It was a beautiful day so we
had a **picnic** in the park.

picnic meal that you eat outside

picture

Josh has painted a
picture of himself.

picture drawing or painting of something

pie

Apple **pie** is one of
my favourite things.

pie baked pastry with a filling

pig

The female **pig** is called a sow.
Baby pigs are called piglets.

pig farm animal with a snout and a little tail

pilot

Sam's dad is a **pilot**.
It is a very important job.

pilot person who flies an aeroplane

pineapple

A **pineapple** has very tough skin,
but the fruit is sweet and juicy.

pineapple large fruit with spiky leaves

planet

Saturn is a very large **planet**
with rings of rock and ice.

planet huge ball of rock that orbits the sun

polar bear

The **polar bear** has very thick
fur to keep him warm.

polar bear very big bear with white fur

present

I wonder what could be inside
this birthday **present**?

present package that you give or receive

pull

Everybody had to **pull** the
rope as hard as possible.

pull to move something towards you

puppies

Tess and Jess are a pair
of playful **puppies**.

puppies baby dogs

push

It was Kerri-Ann's turn
to **push** the pushchair.

push to move something away from you

Qq

queen

Anna was dressed as a
queen for the party.

queen woman who heads a country

quiet

The girls had to be **quiet** because
their baby brother was sleeping.

quiet no noise, or not loud

Rr

rabbit

My pet **rabbit** is called Mabel. She
lives in a hutch in our garden.

rabbit small, furry animal with long ears

race

On sports day I take part
in a running **race**

race competition to see who is fastest

racing car

This **racing car** can go
at about 240 km/h.

racing car car that goes very fast around a track

railway

These trains are running on
a very busy **railway**.

railway track for trains to run along

rain

Melanie loves to go for
a walk in the **rain**.

rain drops of water that fall from the sky

rainbow

I looked up to the sky and
saw a pretty **rainbow**.

rainbow colours made by sun shining through rain

rat

This **rat** is sniffing around
for something to eat.

rat long-tailed rodent, like a large mouse

read

Grace loves to **read** her
books after school.

read to understand the meaning of words

reptile

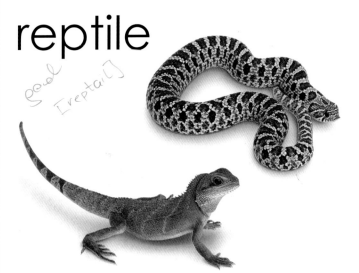

A **reptile** such as a snake or
lizard likes hot weather.

reptile cold-blooded scaly animal

rhinoceros

A **rhinoceros** can run very fast – get
out of the way if you see one!

rhinoceros large, heavy animal with horns

ride

Emma loves to **ride** her
new bicycle.

ride sit on or in something as it moves

right

This arrow is pointing
to the **right**.

right the opposite of left

river

This **river** leads through the
countryside to the sea.

river large stream of water that flows along

road

We drive on this **road**,
to get to school.

road hard track for vehicles to drive on

robot

This **robot** is one of my
favourite toys.

robot machine that can move

rock

We found this **rock** when we
were digging up the garden.

rock large, heavy stone

rocket

The space shuttle uses two very
powerful **rocket** engines.

rocket machine that powers spacecraft

roll

In gym class I learned how
to do a forward **roll**.

roll turn over as you move along

room

Rose is furnishing a **room** in
her new doll's house.

room space in a building

roots

You need to pull up this
plant to see its **roots**.

roots parts of a plant that grow underground

rose

Take care when picking a **rose**
because it has a very thorny stem.

rose sweet-smelling flower with lots of petals

run

I like to go for a **run** during
my school break.

run to move quickly on your legs

Ss

sad

I always feel **sad** at the
end of my holiday.

sad feeling unhappy

same

All of these ducks are the **same**.
How many ducks are there?

same to be exactly like something

sand

The girls enjoyed playing in the **sand** when they went to the beach.

sand small grains of rock on a beach

school

Lewis goes to **school** five days a week.

school place where you go to learn

seagull

A **seagull** will follow a fishing boat, hoping to get some fish.

seagull large grey and white sea bird

seasons

spring

summer

autumn

winter

Each year is divided into four **seasons**.

seasons times of the year

see

School has finished and Jack
can **see** his mummy.

see to look at, or notice something

shadow

Can you point to Skye's
shadow in this picture?

shadow shape made when you stand in light

shampoo

Benedict likes the bubbles
that the **shampoo** makes.

shampoo type of soap used to wash hair

shape

Triangles, squares, circles and
hearts are all types of **shapes**.

shape pattern made by something

shark

The **shark** is one of the world's
most dangerous animals.

shark large sea animal with sharp teeth

sheep

This **sheep** is ready to have
its coat sheared.

sheep farm animal with a woolly coat

shell

Some people say that you can
hear the sea inside a **shell**.

shell hard outside cover of a sea creature

ship

This **ship** carries lots of
passengers on their holidays.

ship large vehicle that sails on the sea

short

Carrie is tall and her brother Craig is **short**.

short not tall, or long

shout

Mark has to **shout** to make himself heard.

shout to speak very loudly

sick

Elliot did not go to school today because he was **sick**.

sick to be unwell

silly

Kylie was being **silly** and she made a funny face.

silly foolish, or not sensible

sing

Amanda likes to **sing** in
the school musicals.

sing make music with your voice

sister

Bethany is Cathy's
younger **sister**.

sister girl with the same parents as you

skateboard

Kieran practised riding his
skateboard every day.

skateboard board with wheels that you ride

sky

Rose looked up and saw an
aeroplane in the **sky**.

sky space above you, where the clouds are

sleep

I like to have at least eight
hours of **sleep** a night.

sleep to close your eyes and rest

snake

This is a Mexican milk **snake**.
It is often seen beside roads.

snake reptile with a long, thin body

sneeze

Aleisha sniffed the flower
and it made her **sneeze**.

sneeze push air through your nose suddenly

snow

In winter when it's cold, the
landscape gets covered in **snow**.

snow small, white flakes of frozen water

soccer

Every Saturday morning,
Max goes to **soccer** practice.

soccer ball game where teams try to score goals

soft

Alice likes to cuddle her
favourite **soft** teddy.

soft not stiff or hard

star

Look at the sky tonight and see
if you can see a shining **star**.

star bright light you see in the sky at night

starfish

You can sometimes find a **starfish**
in a rock pool at the beach.

starfish sea animal with five arms

strawberries

We like to eat **strawberries** with sugar and cream.

strawberries small, red, juicy fruits

sun

In the evening, the sky turns orange as the **sun** starts to set.

sun huge star that the earth orbits

sunglasses

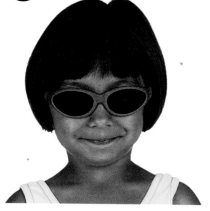

Sally wore her **sunglasses** when she went to the beach.

sunglasses glasses you wear when it is sunny

swim

Sam likes to go for a **swim** every Saturday morning.

swim move yourself through water

Tt

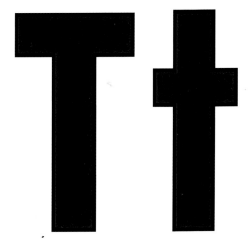

table

The children sat around the **table** to have their lunch.

table furniture with a flat top and legs

talk

On Mondays we like to **talk** about the things we did on the weekend.

talk to speak, have a conversation

teacher

Our geography **teacher** is called
Mrs MacLean.

teacher person who helps you to learn

teeth

Benjamin is pointing
to his **teeth**.

teeth white things in your mouth used to chew

telephone

My sister is always using
the **telephone**.

telephone instrument used to talk to someone

television

Alfie sat down to watch his favourite
programme on **television**.

television machine that shows moving pictures

tennis

Graham's favourite sport is
tennis. He practises every day.

tennis ball game played with a racket

thin

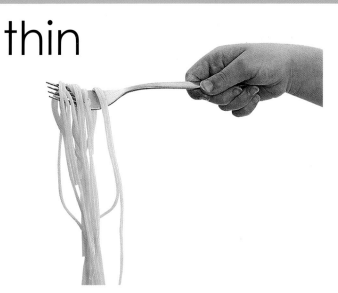

Spaghetti is a very **thin**
type of pasta.

thin not fat or thick

thirsty

Sally had a drink of juice
because she was **thirsty.**

thirsty wanting to drink something

tiger

The **tiger** is a cat that
lives in Asia.

tiger wild cat with orange and black stripes

time

The **time** shown on this
clock is ten to two.

time moment shown on a watch or clock

tired

It had been a very long day,
and Amanda was **tired**.

tired needing rest or sleep

toes

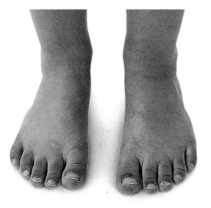

We have ten **toes** –
five on each foot.

toes the parts at the end of your feet

toilet

Oliver uses a step when
he goes to the **toilet**.

toilet place where you get rid of body waste

tomato

The **tomato** is a fruit that
grows on a vine.

tomato round, red fruit eaten in salads

tongue

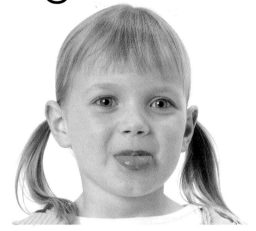

Sarah is sticking her **tongue**
out at her friends.

tongue long, soft part in your mouth

tools

Daddy keeps his **tools** in
a box in the garage.

tools instrument that helps you do a job

toothbrush

It is important to use your **toothbrush**
to brush your teeth twice a day.

toothbrush brush used for cleaning your teeth

top

Jennifer is sitting on
the **top** of the table.

top the highest part of something

toucan

The **toucan** jumps from tree to
tree, eating nuts and seeds.

toucan jungle bird with a large, colourful beak

toys

My teddy and my drum are
my two favourite **toys**.

toys something that you play with

tractor

A **tractor** has big, chunky tyres
to drive through muddy fields.

tractor vehicle used on a farm

train

This **train** runs on the city's
underground railway.

train vehicle that travels along a railway

tree

This **tree** has been growing in
the garden for 50 years.

tree large plant with a thick trunk

truck

This **truck** has a big,
powerful diesel engine.

truck large vehicle that carries goods

trumpet

Graham practised playing his
trumpet every night after school.

trumpet musical instrument made of brass

trunk

The elephant uses its **trunk** to drink, smell and pick things up.

trunk an elephant's long nose

T-shirt

Aleisha has a **T-shirt** with a pretty pattern on the front.

T-shirt piece of clothing with short sleeves

tulips

Tulips are flowers that grow in the spring.

tulips cup-shaped flowers that grow from bulbs

twins

Ian and Simon are identical **twins**. They look exactly like each other.

twins brothers or sisters who are born together

U u

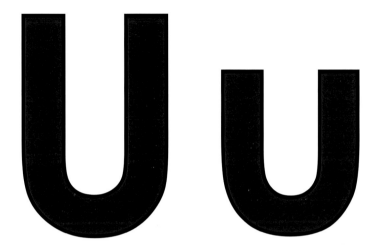

umbrella

This blue and yellow **umbrella** is large enough to hide under.

umbrella object used to keep rain off you

under

Benjamin is hiding **under** the table.

under to be below something

V v

vacuum cleaner

Denise is pretending to clean
up with the **vacuum cleaner**.

vacuum cleaner machine that sucks up dirt

vegetables

Eating a variety of **vegetables**
helps to keep you healthy.

vegetables plants that you can eat

vet

The **vet** checked to see if
Sammy was better.

vet person who looks after sick animals

violin

You play a **violin** by rubbing
a bow across the strings.

violin musical instrument with strings

volcano

Sometimes a **volcano** erupts,
spitting out hot lava and ash.

volcano mountain with a hole in the top

vulture

A **vulture** looks for dead
animals to feed on.

vulture large bird with a bald head

W w

walk

These three penguins are
going for a **walk**.

walk to move along with your feet

wallaby

The **wallaby** has powerful
back legs that help it jump.

wallaby small, furry animal like a kangaroo

walrus

The **walrus** spends most of
its time on the seashore.

walrus large sea animal with long tusks

wash

Lewis always remembers to
wash behind his ears.

wash to clean with soap and water

watch

I checked my **watch** to
see if I was late.

watch device you wear that tells time

water

Amy likes to float on the
water on her raft.

water clear liquid that you drink or swim in

wave

The weekend was over and it was time to **wave** goodbye.

wave to move your hand as a signal

weigh

Cassie had to **weigh** the ingredients for the cake.

weigh to measure the weight of something

wet

Freddie is **wet** because he is in the bath.

wet covered with water

whale

The blue **whale** is the largest animal on earth.

whale large mammal that lives in the sea

wheat

Wheat is grown for its grain.
The grain is used to make bread.

wheat plant grown on a farm

wheel

This is a large **wheel**
from a tractor.

wheel circular object that moves a vehicle

wheelbarrow

I copy my daddy when I play
with my **wheelbarrow**.

wheelbarrow small cart used in a garden

whiskers

Cats use their **whiskers** to feel
for things in front of them.

whiskers long hairs on an animal's face

whisper

Amanda had to **whisper**
her secret to Michael.

whisper to talk very quietly

wind

A very strong **wind** can cause
damage to buildings.

wind air that is moving very quickly

wings

This butterfly has
beautiful, coloured **wings**

wings parts of an animal used to fly

wolf

A **wolf** will howl to call the
other members of its pack.

wolf wild animal like a large dog

wood

Mark went out to collect
more **wood** for the fire.

wood hard part of a tree

wool

Our kitten loves to play
with a ball of **wool**.

wool hair from sheep used to make clothes

world

A map of the **world** shaped
like a ball is called a globe.

world the earth and everything on it

write

Grace is learning to **write** in
her special notebook.

write to put words on paper

X x

X-ray

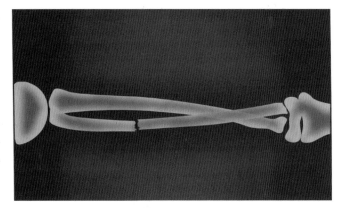

This **X-ray** shows a broken
bone in an arm.

X-ray photograph of the inside of a body

xylophone

Melanie played the **xylophone**
in the school orchestra.

xylophone musical instrument made of bars

Y y

yacht

I like to sail my toy **yacht**
on the lake.

yacht boat with sails

yawn

Louise was feeling very tired
and did a long **yawn**.

yawn to open your mouth and breathe in hard

Zz

zebra

The **zebra** lives on the
plains of Africa.

zebra animal with black and white stripes

zoo

We visited the **zoo** to see the
animals and learn about them

zoo place where wild animals are kept